Original title:
Hearts in Bloom

Author: Swan Charm
ISBN HARDBACK: 978-9916-89-832-1
ISBN PAPERBACK: 978-9916-89-833-8
ISBN EBOOK: 978-9916-89-834-5

Essence of Sacred Growth

In whispers of the dawn's embrace,
The seed of faith begins to race.
With roots that delve in truths so deep,
A promise made, a vow to keep.

Each drop of rain, a blessing sent,
To nurture hearts, pure and content.
In shadows cast by worldly nights,
The spirit blooms in sacred lights.

Through trials fierce, the soul will soar,
Each hurdle crossed, it seeks for more.
The hands that toil, the heart that's pure,
In unity, we find the cure.

The branches stretch towards the skies,
Awakening the spirit's cries.
In harmony with nature's grace,
We journey onward, face to face.

Come gather 'round, the faithful throng,
In shared belief, we all belong.
With every prayer, our essence grows,
In sacred love, the truth bestows.

Blossom the Soul's Yearning

In the garden where hopes reside,
The soul's yearning finds its stride.
Each petal soft, a prayer untold,
In fragrant truth, the spirit unfolds.

Beneath the moon's gentle glow,
The heart ignites, a holy flow.
With each sunrise, it's reborn,
In moments hushed, divinely sworn.

Through valleys low and mountains high,
The spirit dances, wings to fly.
In trials faced, we find our song,
Together we rise, where we belong.

With every heartbeat, whispers speak,
In silence found, our souls to seek.
The bonds of love that cannot sever,
In sacred light, we bloom forever.

So nurture dreams in faith's embrace,
In unity, we share this space.
With open hearts, let kindness flow,
In sacred gardens, let us grow.

Nurturing the Seeds of the Divine

In the heart, a seed is sown,
Each whispered prayer, a gentle tone.
With faith like water, love the light,
We nurture growth through day and night.

In soil rich with hope it lies,
Beneath the sunlit, endless skies.
With gentle hands, we tend the prayer,
United hearts, a bond laid bare.

Together we tend each fragile sprout,
In silence strong, we sing about.
For in our care, new life shall rise,
A testament of love’s great ties.

Through storms and trials, we hold the ground,
In sacred spaces, grace is found.
The seeds of light, we watch them grow,
In gardens blessed, our spirits glow.

With every bloom, our souls take flight,
In colors pure, we share the light.
Nurturing seeds, hand in hand,
In the shadow of the Divine's grand plan.

The Quiet Joy of Blooming Together

In the stillness, our hearts align,
A gentle dance, your hand in mine.
Together we bloom, side by side,
In love's embrace, we shall abide.

Every petal whispers divine,
In unity, our souls entwine.
We find our strength in quiet grace,
In blooming joy, we seek His face.

Through seasons shift, the light shall guide,
In sacred trust, we won't divide.
Each breath we take, a prayer of peace,
In tender moments, doubts will cease.

As flowers burst with colors bright,
Our spirits soar, a shared delight.
In sacred silence, hearts do sing,
The quiet joy that love can bring.

Together, we awaken dreams,
In harmony, life's river streams.
Blooming bright in sacred tether,
We find our path, now and forever.

The Luminous Garden of Belief

In every heart, a garden grows,
With seeds of faith, the spirit knows.
In rows of hope, each thought, a light,
We cultivate through day and night.

Where shadows dance, the truth will shine,
In luminous grace, our souls align.
Together we weed out despair,
In every prayer, love’s fragrant air.

With colors bright, our dreams take root,
In blossom's glow, we find the truth.
The fragrant essence of belief
Brings gentle joy, dispels the grief.

In this garden, hand in hand,
We nurture life, forever planned.
Each leaping flame, our spirits soar,
In unity, the heart finds more.

Together we walk, the path so clear,
In luminous gardens, love draws near.
In belief we thrive, forever blessed,
A luminous life, in faith confessed.

Sacred Colors of Affection's Labors

In shades of love, our hearts displayed,
A tapestry of prayers conveyed.
Each color born from toil and care,
In sacred bonds, our spirits share.

The red of passion, warm and bright,
The blue of peace, a calm delight.
In every hue, a story told,
Of affection's labors, brave and bold.

In golden rays, we find our way,
Through trials faced, come what may.
With every stroke, we paint the love,
A divine masterpiece from above.

In labor's love, our hands are worn,
Yet in the struggle, hope is born.
We gather strength in colors rare,
In sacred art, our hearts laid bare.

Together we weave, both strong and free,
In sacred colors, a unity.
In affection's labor, we shall thrive,
As sacred hearts continue alive.

Sacred Threads in Nature’s Fabric

In the whisper of the breeze, we find,
A sacred thread that binds us all,
Each leaf a testament divine,
Nature's hymn in twilight's call.

The river flows with grace and might,
A mirror of our souls' deep yearn,
Reflecting stars that guide at night,
In silence, we together learn.

Mountains rise, a grand embrace,
Their majesty speaks of His love,
In every shadow, every space,
The hand of God from high above.

The flowers bloom in vibrant hues,
A palette of His endless grace,
Each petal sings, a soft muse,
In beauty, we behold His face.

As seasons change, a sacred dance,
Life cycles in a holy thread,
In every ending there's a chance,
For new beginnings, warmly spread.

Blossoming Affection

In soft twilight, two hearts entwine,
Their whispers float on evening air,
A bond that grows, a love divine,
In every glance, a sacred prayer.

Like blooming roses in the sun,
Their petals curled with tender care,
Each heartbeat knows, they're not alone,
Their spirits rise, an answered dare.

Through trials faced and storms embraced,
Their roots go deep in trusting earth,
In every challenge, love is traced,
A testament of endless worth.

With every dawn, their love does shine,
A golden promise, rich and pure,
In each embrace, they redefine,
What it means to hold the cure.

Together they find joy anew,
In laughter shared, a dance of grace,
In every moment, love breaks through,
A sacred bond no time can erase.

Nature's Sacred Testimony

The whispering trees, they testify,
Of secrets held in ancient wood,
With every rustle, every sigh,
Nature speaks, as she so should.

The mountains stand as witnesses,
To love that spans eternity,
In soaring heights, we find our peace,
A glimpse of heaven, wild and free.

The oceans' waves, a rhythmic beat,
Each crash, a hymn, each ebb, a prayer,
In harmony, our spirits meet,
Their sacred song, a love affair.

The skies adorned with hues of gold,
In sunset's glow, we find our path,
With every dawn, new stories told,
A testament to love's own wrath.

In every creature, great and small,
The spirit dwells, and love resides,
Nature's dance, a sacred call,
Round every corner, grace abides.

Seeds of Trust in the Soil of Love

In gentle hands, the seeds are sown,
With trust that blossoms through the years,
In love's embrace, we're never lone,
Together facing all our fears.

The soil rich with whispered dreams,
A garden where our spirits thrive,
Each sprout a sign of love's moonbeams,
In unity, our hearts revive.

When storms may come and shadows cast,
The roots run deep, entwined as one,
In faith, we rise, through trials passed,
Our love, a bright and steadfast sun.

Through seasons' change, our bond grows strong,
With every sunset, dawn anew,
In nature's choir, we sing our song,
Of trust that flourishes like dew.

In harvest time, we gather round,
The fruits of love, a rich reward,
In every silence, joy is found,
A testament to love's sweet accord.

Blossoms of Faithful Yearning

In the garden of hopes, we stand,
Petals whispering soft, divine plan.
Faith blooms brightly in morning's light,
Guided by grace, we soar in flight.

Hearts entwined in sacred embrace,
Each prayer a step in holy space.
With every breath, we seek the truth,
In woven dreams, we find our youth.

Though shadows loom, our spirits rise,
In trials faced, love never dies.
The sun may set, yet hope will gleam,
In faithful yearning, we dare to dream.

Voices lift in harmonious song,
In unity, we are ever strong.
Together we nurture this seedling fate,
In this sacred bond, we celebrate.

Let blossoms bloom in endless grace,
Filling the world with love's sweet trace.
In faith's embrace, we find our way,
Guided by light, come what may.

The Sanctuary of Love's Harvest

Beneath the arch of heaven's dome,
Where hearts converge, we build our home.
In the quietude of shared delight,
Love's bounty shines, a beacon bright.

Each moment cherished, every glance,
In sacred trust, our souls enhance.
With open hands, we gather grace,
A harvest sweet in love's embrace.

In the stillness, we hear the call,
To lift each other, never fall.
Through laughter shared and burdens eased,
In love's sanctuary, we are pleased.

With every season, joy unfolds,
As stories shared become retold.
In the warmth of kinship's glow,
Together, we learn, together we grow.

Embrace the dawn with hearts so pure,
In love's harvest, we find our cure.
Through trials faced and dreams redeemed,
In sanctuary's arms, we are deemed.

Graceful Tendrils of Trust

In the woven strands of time, we bind,
Graceful tendrils, our hearts aligned.
Through storms that threaten, we hold fast,
In trust's embrace, we're free at last.

Each whispered prayer, a tender thread,
Connecting souls, where love is spread.
We gather strength from every plea,
In faith's assurance, we're set free.

In gentle smiles, we seek the dawn,
Together forged, we carry on.
With open hearts, we pave the way,
In trust's sweet promise, we shall stay.

Though mountains rise and rivers flow,
In each other, we find the glow.
For like the vine that climbs so high,
In love's pure trust, we reach the sky.

As leaves embrace the morning dew,
In fragile moments, we start anew.
With graceful tendrils, intertwined,
In trust's embrace, together we find.

Divine Spirit in Full Flourish

In the quiet breath of morning's grace,
The divine spirit begins to trace.
With each soft sigh, creation sings,
In full flourish, life ever brings.

As sunlight dapples through the trees,
Nature whispers secrets on the breeze.
In every blossom, a story told,
In vibrant hues, our hearts unfold.

Through trials faced, we know the light,
In shadows cast, our souls ignite.
With faith as shelter, love will bloom,
In divine spirit, there's no gloom.

In each heartbeat, a rhythm pure,
The essence of life, forever sure.
In endless cycles, our spirits dance,
In divine embrace, we find our chance.

So let the world in wonder gaze,
At love's reflection in gentle ways.
With every breath, we rise and soar,
In divine spirit, forevermore.

Blooms of Eternal Connection

In gardens lush and green, we find,
The whispers of His love divine.
Each bloom, a testament to grace,
A silent prayer in sacred space.

Through petals soft, His mercy glows,
A bond that in our hearts bestows.
With every fragrance, sweet and pure,
Eternal hope, forever sure.

The colors blend, a vibrant tie,
Reminding us, we cannot die.
In nature's arms, His presence near,
Our spirits rise, dispelling fear.

As seasons shift, the blooms renew,
Each blossom kissed by morning dew.
Together in this holy dance,
We share the joy, we take the chance.

So let us cherish life’s embrace,
In every flower, we find His grace.
A cycle bound, yet ever free,
In blooms of love, we’re meant to be.

Divine Renewal Through Nature

In shaded groves where sunlight breaks,
The trees, they rise, the spirit wakes.
With branches high, they praise the day,
While whispers of His love display.

The river flows, a sacred song,
Each ripple beats, where we belong.
In drops of rain, His kindness falls,
Stirring life in verdant halls.

When blossoms bloom in vibrant hues,
They mirror grace in daily views.
As petals unfurl to greet the sun,
We're drawn to Him, and all is one.

This earth reflects His wondrous art,
In every leaf, we play our part.
So let us seek the truth in light,
With open hearts, embrace the night.

For in each season, breath anew,
The sacred trust of Love shines through.
Through nature's path, we're called to roam,
In divine renewal, we find home.

Petals Reaching for Light

In dawn’s embrace, the flowers wake,
With open hands, their souls partake.
They lift their heads to skies above,
In silent quest for endless love.

Each petal soft, a gentle plea,
To join the dance of harmony.
In sunlight’s glow, they find their way,
A testament to hope's bright ray.

They sway with grace, a sacred trust,
Awakening hearts in dreamers' dust.
In fragrant blooms, the spirit speaks,
A symphony that softly peaks.

Through life, they learn to bend and sway,
To face the storms and find their way.
In every hue, they brightly share,
The light of God, they breathe in air.

So let us be like flowers bold,
Reaching for light, our stories told.
With every bloom, our faith ignites,
Petals of hope, in endless flights.

The Floral Covenant

In sacred bonds, the petals weave,
A tapestry of faith we cleave.
Each bloom a promise, pure and bright,
A covenant sealed in love's own light.

Through fragrant fields, His whispers spread,
In every flower, His spirit led.
With colors bold, they tell the tale,
Of grace that thrives where shadows pale.

As seasons change, the blooms unite,
In harmony, they share their plight.
Together strong, their roots embrace,
A testament to love’s sweet grace.

With gentle rains, the earth will sigh,
Nurtured by tears of the sky.
In every petal, a prayer sown,
In the floral pact, we’re never alone.

So let us honor this sacred vow,
In gratitude, we humbly bow.
For in each bloom, we then can see,
The floral covenant, you and me.

The Prayerful Lotus of Love

In still waters, the lotus blooms,
Whispers of hope in fragrant rooms.
Each petal lifted in humble prayer,
A dance of faith in the silent air.

Beneath the surface, it gently grows,
Reaching for light where the river flows.
In the heart's depth, true love ignites,
A beacon of warmth on the darkest nights.

With every breath, a sacred vow,
To cherish the joy of the here and now.
Petals unfolding to the skies above,
Embracing the world with a heart of love.

In harmony’s song, all souls unite,
A tapestry woven in radiant light.
Together they rise, like the dawn so bright,
The lotus stands tall, a beautiful sight.

In its pure grace, we find our way,
Guided by love, come what may.
Let thoughts of peace be ever near,
In the prayerful lotus, we conquer fear.

Fragrance of Eternal Devotion

In the heart's garden, blooms a rose,
With petals soft, the spirit knows.
Each scent a whisper of love divine,
In the stillness, the soul aligns.

Through trials faced and shadows cast,
The fragrance lingers, steadfast.
A promise woven in every breath,
Devotion's light conquers death.

With every tear, a seed is sown,
The fragrance of love in every tone.
In the quiet, the heart will sing,
Of boundless grace in all things.

In azure skies, the spirit flies,
Embracing truth, where wisdom lies.
Together we rise, united and strong,
In the fragrance of devotion, we all belong.

This sacred bond, a radiant flame,
In each heart's echo, love's sweet name.
Let us cherish and deeply feel,
The fragrance of love, eternal and real.

Nurtured by the Hands of Hope

In gentle hands, the seeds are laid,
With every promise, the soul's cascade.
Nurtured softly, like morning dew,
Hope's embrace whispers anew.

Through storms and trials, we grow tall,
With roots entwined, we shall not fall.
In every struggle, growth unfolds,
A tale of courage, yet untold.

When shadows linger and doubts appear,
The hands of hope draw us near.
In every heartbeat, love's refrain,
We find our strength through joy and pain.

Blooming flowers from darkest clay,
Hope nurtured through night to day.
With open hearts, we share the light,
In unity, we banish night.

Let every seed of kindness grow,
A testament of love we sow.
For in the hands of hope, we find,
A garden rich for all mankind.

Celestial Garden of Grace

Beneath the stars, a garden lies,
Where each flower reaches for the skies.
A tapestry of colors bright,
In the celestial garden, pure delight.

With every dawn, new blooms arise,
Touched by warmth, where beauty flies.
In the gentle breeze, a sacred hymn,
As nature breathes, the spirit swims.

The trees stand tall, guardians of peace,
In their embrace, all sorrows cease.
In quiet moments, hearts commune,
Under the glow of the silver moon.

With every petal, a story told,
Of love and grace that never grows old.
In unity's dance, we celebrate,
The celestial garden, our shared fate.

So let us cherish this sacred space,
Where every heart finds its place.
In the celestial garden, forever we race,
In the arms of grace, we find our face.

Serenity Among the Fragrant Blooms

In gardens green where stillness reigns,
The fragrant blooms lift hearts from pains.
They whisper peace in gentle sighs,
And call the soul to rise and rise.

The sun-kissed petals, soft and bright,
Reflect the love of morning light.
In this embrace of nature's grace,
We find our refuge, our sacred space.

Each flower tells a tale divine,
Of hope and faith, in roots entwined.
They dance with breezes, pure and free,
Uniting all in harmony.

As fragrant scents drift through the air,
We breathe in blessings, sacred prayer.
With every bloom, our spirits soar,
In gratitude, forevermore.

So let us tend this garden fair,
With kindness sewn in every care.
In every petal, see the sign,
That in this life, the blooms are thine.

The Hallelujah of Blossoming Souls

In quiet woods where shadows play,
The souls of flowers find their way.
They lift their heads with fervent joy,
Singing praises without employ.

With every bud, a song unfolds,
A melody of love retold.
The vibrant hues, a sacred light,
That fills the heart with pure delight.

Through trials faced and storms endured,
In blossomed grace, our hearts assured.
For every soul, a chance to shine,
Together, entwined in love divine.

The winds of faith will guide our flight,
In gardens rich with spirit's might.
With every blossom, we are whole,
Hallelujah echoes in our soul.

So let us dance in unity,
With every petal, let it be.
In gratitude for life’s sweet song,
We sing our hallelujahs strong.

Cherished Buds of Spirituality

In sacred spaces where we dwell,
The cherished buds begin to swell.
Their colors bright, a vision clear,
Awakening the heart’s true sphere.

Each gentle leaf, a heart's embrace,
Reminds us of the sacred race.
In every whisper of the wind,
A promise bound, our souls rescind.

These buds of faith, so tender, bloom,
Dispelling darkness, bringing gloom.
In their unfolding, love will rise,
A testament to the skies.

With every petal, truth is found,
In silent moments, hearts unbound.
Cherished gifts from realms above,
In every bud, we find our love.

So cultivate this garden dear,
With every thought and every tear.
For in the soil of deep belief,
We nurture seeds of sweet relief.

Petals of Compassionate Light

In twilight's glow, the petals gleam,
With compassionate light, they beam.
Each color soft, a warm embrace,
Inviting all to find their place.

Beneath the branches, shadows cast,
We feel the love that's meant to last.
Through every bloom, a gentle hand,
Lifts up the weary, takes a stand.

Amidst the strife, these petals shine,
A legacy of love divine.
In every heart, a light ignites,
Embracing all in tender rights.

With every breath, compassion grows,
A garden vast where kindness flows.
Petals scattered on the ground,
Remind us all, love knows no bound.

So let us gather in this space,
With open hearts and warm embrace.
For in the light of every flower,
We find our strength, our finest hour.

Sowing Seeds of Hope

In fields of light we cast our dreams,
With gentle hands and hearts that gleam.
Each seed we plant in faith anew,
Sprouts visions bright, a promise true.

The sun above, a guiding grace,
Nurtures each tender, sacred space.
As rain descends, we find our song,
In harmony, we all belong.

Through trials faced, we hold our ground,
In every leaf, His love is found.
With joy we gather, share our yield,
In valleys low and open field.

With strife will come the sweetest bloom,
In darkness found, we light the room.
Our trust in Him, a steadfast root,
From barren soil, life's hopes compute.

So let us sow, with bold embrace,
The seeds of hope in every place.
Together rise, in faith we'll stand,
A harvest rich from holy land.

Flourishing in Faith

In whispered prayers, our spirits soar,
A gentle breeze, God's open door.
With every step, our trust grows wide,
In faith we flourish, side by side.

The mountains high, the valleys deep,
In truth we walk, His promise keep.
Against all odds, our spirits weave,
In every challenge, we believe.

With open hearts, we share the load,
Together on this sacred road.
Through storms we pass, yet never stray,
In light we find the stronger way.

Each moment blessed, a chance to grace,
To see His love in every face.
In kindness shown, our hearts align,
Together, in His word we shine.

So let us rise, in unity,
A beacon bright for all to see.
Flourishing in faith, we stand tall,
In love's embrace, we conquer all.

The Beauty of Sacred Spaces

In sacred spaces, calm and still,
We seek the light, a higher will.
With open hearts, we gather near,
In every moment, feel Him here.

The laughter shared, the tears we shed,
In love's embrace, our spirits fed.
A choir of faith, our voices blend,
In harmony, our worries mend.

The candles burn, their glow divine,
In every heart, His love we find.
Through songs of joy, our praises rise,
A sacred bond beneath the skies.

And when we part, we carry on,
The beauty found, the love, the song.
In every step, we hold Him close,
In sacred spaces, we find hope.

For life itself, a holy grace,
In every heart, a sacred place.
Together, we embrace the call,
To share His love, with one and all.

Love's Blooming Testament

In every heart, love takes its root,
A blooming flower, pure and astute.
With kindness shared, and hands entwined,
In love’s embrace, our souls aligned.

For every smile, a light we bring,
In joy we gather, voices sing.
With open arms, we hold the weak,
In love’s sweet words, His truth we speak.

Through trials faced, we come alive,
In unity, the hope we strive.
With gentle hands, we sow the seed,
In love’s testament, we find our creed.

With patience shown, and faith aglow,
In every heart, His love will grow.
Together we rise, as one we stand,
In love's blooming testament, hand in hand.

So let us shine, and be the light,
In every darkness, share the sight.
For love's embrace, our truest quest,
In service found, we are the blessed.

The Harvest of Kindred Spirits

In fields where whispers softly blend,
Hearts gather close, their souls ascend.
Together, under Heaven's gaze,
They nurture dreams through endless days.

With hands entwined, they lift their praise,
As echoes of their laughter raise.
Each kindness sown within the earth,
Awaits a bloom, a sacred birth.

The thread of love, so finely spun,
Connects us all, we are as one.
In shared abundance, hope ignites,
Our spirits glow with stars so bright.

Beneath the boughs where shadows play,
Together, we embrace the day.
In every heart, a season grows,
For kindness is the life that flows.

So gather here, in sacred space,
In unity, we find our grace.
The harvest ripe, our souls entwined,
In love's embrace, true peace we find.

Tenderest Vows in Full Bloom

With petals soft and fragrance sweet,
Two souls unite, their hearts entreat.
In sacred vows, their pledge is shared,
In gentle whispers, love declared.

Through stormy skies and sunny days,
Their bond endures, in hopeful ways.
Each moment cherished, faces bright,
Together they walk towards the light.

In gardens lush where blessings flow,
The seeds of trust begin to grow.
Their laughter weaves a tapestry,
Of tender vows, eternally.

With every glance, their spirits soar,
In union strong, they seek for more.
Through trials faced, their hearts align,
In love, they bloom, a sacred sign.

As blossoms dance in evening's grace,
They stand as one, in warm embrace.
Through seasons vast, their love will thrive,
In tenderest vows, they are alive.

The Celestial Embrace of Nature’s Love

In twilight’s hush, where angels sigh,
The stars above begin to cry.
With every breeze, a gentle touch,
Nature's love reveals so much.

Amongst the trees, the whispers flow,
In every leaf, the heartbeats grow.
In sacred space, all life doth roam,
Through nature's arms, we find our home.

The rivers sing, the mountains stand,
In beauty forged by Heaven's hand.
Each creature walks, a path divine,
In the embrace, their souls entwine.

With every dawn, hope’s promise glows,
As petals open, tenderness shows.
Together we breathe in the grace,
Of nature's love, our sacred place.

So let us roam through fields of dreams,
Embraced by love in silver streams.
In harmony, we come alive,
With nature's love, our spirits thrive.

Seraphic Blossoms of Grace

In gardens where the angels play,
The blossoms bloom in soft array.
Seraphic light caresses each,
A sacred love, so pure to teach.

With every petal, stories rise,
Of faith and hope beneath the skies.
In unity, they softly sway,
In grace, the heart begins to pray.

Reflected in the morning dew,
A promise made, forever true.
Through trials faced and joy embraced,
In every moment, love is traced.

The fragrance dances on the breeze,
A symphony of life that frees.
In every sigh, a blessing drawn,
An echo of the coming dawn.

So let our spirits rise and twine,
In seraph's glow, our hearts align.
With every step, we find our place,
In seraphic blossoms, we embrace.

Spiritual Petal Paths

In gardens where the prayer blooms,
Gentle whispers fill the air.
Each petal holds a sacred truth,
Guiding souls to show they care.

The sun bestows its golden light,
Upon the paths we walk with grace.
In every shade, His love shines bright,
Reflecting hope in every place.

With every step, the heart finds peace,
As winds of faith begin to stir.
The spirit dances, joys increase,
In fragrant moments, we confer.

So tread these paths with reverent hearts,
Embrace the silence and the song.
For every bloom, a soul's new start,
In unity, we all belong.

Let gratitude be like the dew,
Resting soft on every leaf.
In every petal, love rings true,
A sacred promise beyond grief.

Sanctified Blooms of Devotion

Through sacred fields, our hearts entwine,
Petals raised in joyful prayer.
Each fragrance whispers, 'You are mine,'
In devotion woven rare.

The colors dance in gentle sway,
A tapestry of holy light.
In every bud, a vow to stay,
Within the soft embrace of night.

Let every bloom remind our souls,
Of love that's pure, of grace divine.
In gardens vast, where spirit rolls,
We seek the path, the grand design.

Amidst the thorns, our faith shall grow,
Reaching high to touch the skies.
In every petal, love will flow,
As devotion's song replies.

With hands uplifted, hearts will sing,
Of sanctified blooms, hope's delight.
In every dawn, fresh blessings bring,
The sacred truth in morning light.

Blossoming Faith

In fields of grace, our spirits rise,
Where blossoms open wide in trust.
Each petal mirrors heaven's sighs,
A testament to love robust.

With every dew that graces bloom,
We find the strength to carry on.
In fragrant whispers, in the room,
Hope is reborn with every dawn.

Each flower tells of trials faced,
Of storms that passed, of shadows cast.
Yet here in sunlight, hearts embraced,
In faith we find our shadows past.

As petals fall and seasons change,
Our hearts, like gardens, grow anew.
Through faith’s embrace, we find exchange,
In beauty’s light, our spirits grew.

So let us tend these sacred seeds,
With love as rich as earth's own clay.
In blossoming faith, our heart concedes,
To walk the path, come what may.

Nectar of the Divine

In every flower, a drop of grace,
Sweet nectar flowing from above.
A taste of God's warm, soft embrace,
In every petal, purest love.

We gather round with open hearts,
To sip the blessings shared so sweet.
In every smile, the spirit starts,
To weave a bond where souls can meet.

The garden sings a sacred song,
Each note a prayer, each breath a plea.
In unity, we all belong,
In sacred harmony, we're free.

As bees collect, so shall we feed,
On nectar rich with faith's delight.
In every moment, plant the seed,
Of love and joy, in darkest night.

So walk with me in fields of light,
With every step, let spirits soar.
For in this dance, the world feels right,
The nectar of the Divine we pour.

Petal-Kissed Blessings of Loyalty

In the garden where hopes entwine,
Petals softly whisper divine,
Each bloom a promise to uphold,
With roots of loyalty, brave and bold.

Through trials of time, we stand as one,
Guided by light of the faithful sun,
In shadows deep, our spirits rise,
In every prayer, a bond defies.

With every dawn, our hearts renew,
As petals fall, love's strength shines through,
We honor vows, steadfast and true,
In every kiss, a sacred hue.

In the sacred breeze, our voices soar,
Bound together, forever more,
With gratitude for this grace bestowed,
Petal-kissed blessings on our road.

In gratitude, we lift our song,
For loyalty that makes us strong,
With faith as our guide, together we'll roam,
In this garden, we find our home.

Flourishing in Divine Time

In silence, we seek the sacred flow,
As seasons change, our spirits grow,
With each heartbeat, we know it's fate,
Flourishing in love, we celebrate.

The hands of time weave a gentle thread,
Of patience and faith in the lives we've led,
Through trials faced beneath heaven's gaze,
In divine time, we find our ways.

With eyes raised high to the stars above,
We gather strength, through endless love,
In every moment, the truth ignites,
Guided by grace, our soul unites.

As blossoms greet the morning light,
We walk together, hearts so bright,
In the promise of dawn, we find our path,
In a world of faith, beyond all wrath.

In dance of time, we understand,
That love forever holds our hands,
With each step forward, our spirits climb,
Flourishing always in divine time.

The Holy Blossom of Committed Bonds

In gardens lush where the spirit glows,
A holy blossom in devotion grows,
Petal by petal, our hearts entwined,
In sacred bonds, our souls aligned.

Each promise shared, a fragrant breath,
In love's embrace, we conquer death,
With roots that dig in the earth so deep,
We harvest joys that forever keep.

As seasons change, our spirits bloom,
In unity's light, we dispel the gloom,
Each day we nurture this gift divine,
In the garden of love, our hearts combine.

Through storms that come and shadows that fade,
In every trial, our faith displayed,
With blossoms bright, our dreams ascend,
In committed bonds, we find our friend.

With every prayer, our souls take flight,
In the holy blossom, we find the light,
Together we flourish, hand in hand,
In love's embrace, forever we stand.

Arising from the Soil of Faith

From soil rich with purpose and grace,
We rise together, an endless chase,
In faith we stand, our roots secure,
Arising strong, steadfast and pure.

With every drop of rain that falls,
The whispers of love's gentle calls,
In unity, we weather the storm,
With hope as our guide, forever warm.

In the warmth of the sun, our spirits bloom,
Dispelling the darkness, we share our room,
Together we journey, hearts ablaze,
In faith's embrace, we sing our praise.

As blossoms open in radiant light,
We honor the journey, day and night,
Each petal a story, each stem a prayer,
In the soil of faith, we lay our care.

In sacred trust, we cultivate love,
With blessings sent from above,
Arising as one, forever we'll stand,
In the soil of faith, hand in hand.

Petals of the Covenant

In the garden of grace, we kneel and pray,
Petals fall softly, guiding our way.
Each bloom a promise, a sacred sign,
Whispers of love, the divine intertwine.

The sun smiles down on the fruitful ground,
In harmony, hearts, and hopes abound.
Together we gather, in faith we unite,
The colors of trust, a heavenly light.

Winds carry prayers to the heavens above,
Each petal a token of God's endless love.
With roots entwined in soil so pure,
Our spirits awaken, safe and secure.

Through trials and storms, we stand so tall,
In petals of promise, we find our call.
A tapestry woven with threads of grace,
In covenant's arms, we embrace our place.

Beneath the vast sky, the stars brightly shine,
A testament strong, the universe divine.
Together we flourish, a garden we share,
Petals of the covenant, bloom everywhere.

The Divine Blossom

Beneath the heavens, where the angels sing,
The divine blossom bears each sacred thing.
With fragrant whispers and silken light,
It teaches the heart to seek the right.

In shadows it grows, through hope and despair,
A beacon of faith, a promise laid bare.
Each petal a lesson, each stem a prayer,
In nature's embrace, we find solace there.

The roots drink deeply from love's gentle stream,
Awakening spirits, igniting the dream.
Together we flourish, hand in hand,
In the garden of God, forever we stand.

Time dances lightly through every glade,
In the chorus of life, our voices cascade.
The divine blossom sings with sweet grace,
A hymn of the heart, in this sacred space.

As seasons change, still we remain bound,
In the beauty of faith, pure love is found.
The divine blossom, our eternal song,
Guiding us gently, where we all belong.

Spiritual Tendrils of Hope

In the silence of night, hope's tendrils rise,
Connecting our souls to the vast, starry skies.
Each whisper of faith, like a breeze that stirs,
Life flows through our spirits, in gentle purrs.

With roots in the earth, our dreams take flight,
Awakening love in the soft morning light.
Together we journey through shadow and shine,
In the tendrils of hope, our hearts align.

When trials surround us, when doubts seem so deep,
Spiritual tendrils hold fast, never sleep.
They weave through the darkness, ignite every spark,
In the embrace of love, we banish the dark.

Each tendril a prayer, each leaf a song,
In unity's garden, we ever belong.
The pulse of creation flows bright and free,
Spiritual tendrils unite you and me.

Beneath the broad canopy, we share our dreams,
In the dance of existence, nothing's as it seems.
With each step we take, our spirits will rise,
Tendrils of hope in the vast, endless skies.

Nature's Testament of Love

In petals and leaves, nature sings her song,
A testament of love, vivid and strong.
With rivers of grace, her bounty flows wide,
In every embrace, the universe abides.

Mountains stand tall, reaching for the skies,
In whispers of trees, our spirit replies.
The sun's golden kiss, the moon's silver glow,
Nature's testament flourishes, steady does grow.

Through valleys and fields, the seasons unfold,
Stories of love, in silence retold.
Each heartbeat of earth, a sacred refrain,
In nature's pure arms, love’s wisdom remains.

With stars like witnesses, glittering bright,
Nature cradles dreams, through day and through night.
Her gentle caress, a promise to keep,
In nature's testament, our souls will leap.

So gather in peace, beneath wide-spread skies,
In nature's embrace, true love never dies.
A circle of life, forever we weave,
Nature's testament, in joy, we believe.

Sacred Colors of Creation

In the dawn's embrace, colors arise,
Whispers of grace beneath azure skies.
Each hue a promise, each shade a song,
In the tapestry of life, we all belong.

The crimson of love, the gold of light,
Together they weave, dispelling the night.
Emerald fields of faith stretch wide,
In every heart, the Creator's guide.

Violet dreams in the twilight glow,
Soft pastels where the gentle winds blow.
Nature's palette, a sacred delight,
Reflecting the glory of day and night.

The ocean's blues tell tales of grace,
Each wave a moment, a sacred space.
In the mountains high, where the spirits soar,
Creation speaks softly, forevermore.

With every color, a story unfolds,
In the arms of silence, the truth beholds.
Reverence for beauty, humble and pure,
In the sacred creation, we all endure.

Blooming Through Trials

In the shadows deep, where sorrow dwells,
Hope takes root, and spirit swells.
Through stormy skies and raging seas,
A bloom emerges, carried by the breeze.

Each thorn a lesson, each petal a prayer,
Strength in the struggle, love everywhere.
From ashes to beauty, the journey we trace,
In every hardship, we find His grace.

The fragrance of faith in the darkest hour,
A beacon of light, a sacred flower.
With every petal, we rise and stand,
With hands lifted high, united we band.

In gardens of trials, the blossoms grow,
Bearing witness to the heavy hearts we know.
As seasons shift and life does unfold,
In the tapestry of time, love takes hold.

So let us bloom where the trials reside,
In the warmth of His love, forever our guide.
Each florid testament, a story divine,
In the bloom of our hearts, His promise will shine.

The Language of Divine Flowers

In the whispering winds, flowers converse,
Secrets of heavens in petals diverse.
Each blossom a prayer, a silent decree,
Speaking the truths of eternity.

The rose, a symbol of love so pure,
In its fragrant embrace, we feel secure.
Lilies of peace in the meadows wide,
Tell tales of solace where hearts can abide.

Daisies of joy with faces so bright,
Dancing in the sun, basking in light.
In each vibrant hue, a story is spun,
The language of flowers, united as one.

In gardens divine, where spirits entwine,
Every flower a verse, forever a sign.
The tulips of faith, the violets of grace,
In the heart's own garden, we find our place.

Let us cherish the blooms that nature has wrought,
In every petal, a message is caught.
Through the vibrant language, our souls can soar,
In the divine silence, hear the flowers implore.

Divine Designs in Nature

In the intricate dance of leaf and vine,
Nature reveals a design so divine.
With every sunrise, a canvas anew,
Crafted by hands of grace, ever true.

Mountains stand tall, a testament bold,
Guardians of stories, ancient and old.
Rivers of wisdom flow deep from the heart,
In nature's embrace, we each play a part.

The stars in the heavens, a cosmic decree,
Mapping out destinies, wild and free.
In seasons of change, every cycle maintains,
The whispers of purpose in life's gentle reigns.

Flora and fauna, a woven delight,
Each thread a reminder of grace and light.
In patterns of beauty, creation unfolds,
The divine designs in stories untold.

May we wander in awe of the world’s grand scheme,
In every small detail, a heavenly dream.
In nature’s design, we find our way home,
In the heart of creation, together we roam.

The Symphony of Flourishing Emotions

In the heart where spirit plays,
Whispers of joy find their ways,
Each tear a note, a sacred sound,
In harmony, our souls are found.

Gratitude blooms like morning light,
Chasing shadows of the night,
In every breath, a prayer we sing,
As hope and faith take gentle wing.

With trials faced, our hearts align,
In love's embrace, we brightly shine,
Resilience grows from seeds of grace,
Through darkest paths, we find our place.

The symphony of life unfolds,
In stories of the brave and bold,
Together, we transcend the pain,
In unity, our hearts remain.

So let us dance in joy divine,
In this sacred path, we intertwine,
For every emotion, a note of peace,
In love's embrace, our souls release.

Blooming Under Sacred Skies

Under skies where whispers dwell,
Each petal tells a tale to tell,
In gardens rich with love's embrace,
Blooming hearts find their rightful place.

Morning dew, a blessing sent,
Awakens life with sweet content,
Sunlight pours, a golden grace,
Kissing blooms, time's tender trace.

In sacred moments, silence speaks,
Each gentle breath, the soul it seeks,
With every bud and every seed,
Life's promise flows, a sacred creed.

Nurtured by the hands of faith,
We grow like flowers, bright and wraith,
In harmonious, divine embrace,
We thrive beneath the sacred space.

So let our voices rise in song,
A chorus where our hearts belong,
Together, in this sacred sky,
We bloom in love, our spirits high.

Love’s Luminous Growth

From tiny seeds, our love does rise,
Reaching toward the endless skies,
Each heartbeat marks the moments passed,
In sacred light, our shadows cast.

With gentle hands, we tend the soil,
In trust, we nourish love's sweet toil,
Through storms and sun, we learn to sway,
In every breath, we find our way.

As seasons change, our roots grow deep,
In love’s embrace, our dreams we keep,
Through trials fierce, we stand attire,
In unity, our souls aspire.

Luminous stillness in the night,
Guides us with its soft, warm light,
Together, reaching for the stars,
In love’s embrace, we conquer scars.

Forever bound by faith’s sweet kiss,
In every moment, find our bliss,
Love’s sacred growth, a precious thread,
In harmony, our spirits wed.

The Sacred Field of Embodied Love

Across the field where spirits meet,
In sacred unity, love’s heartbeat,
Each whispered prayer, a gentle guide,
In embodied grace, we abide.

With open hearts, we weave the light,
In every soul, a spark ignites,
One body joined in love’s embrace,
Transforming lives, a sacred space.

In every glance, a story told,
In kindness shared, our hearts unfold,
Together, we cultivate the earth,
In love’s pure grace, we find our worth.

With patience as our guiding star,
We journey forth, no matter how far,
Through trials faced, we rise anew,
In sacred fields, our love shines through.

So let us walk this path as one,
In every heartbeat, truth begun,
For in this sacred field, we find,
The essence of love, pure and blind.

Celestial Petals of Peace

In gardens bright with sacred light,
Petals drift on winds of grace.
Each whisper soft, a prayer alight,
Harmony in nature's face.

Clouds above, like angels sing,
A melody of purest love.
Through every heart, their blessings bring,
Transcending realm from skies above.

Golden rays through branches weave,
A tapestry of dreams untold.
In silence deep, we dare believe,
That peace within is ours to hold.

Oh, gentle stream, your waters flow,
Refresh the soul, renew our sight.
In tranquil depths, we come to know,
Divine reflections of the light.

Embrace the path where spirits meet,
In quietude, the heart shall soar.
Celestial petals, pure and sweet,
Awakening peace forevermore.

Awakening the Spirit

When morning dew adorns the rose,
Awakens souls to love anew.
Each petal's blush, the heart bestows,
A sacred promise, ever true.

In stillness, find the holy breath,
Gentle whispers call us near.
Through trials faced, through life and death,
The spirit's hymn becomes so clear.

With every dawn, the shadows fade,
Revealing light in every heart.
Transcending fears that hope delayed,
Together, we shall have a part.

In nature's arms, our souls take flight,
Bathed in love, we seek and find.
Awakening the spirit's light,
In unity, our hearts aligned.

Let gratitude be our refrain,
For every drop of morning rain.
With every moment, grace we gain,
As love transcends the earthly pain.

Blossoms of Transcendence

In twilight's glow, the blossoms bloom,
A symphony of colors bright.
They share with us the sweet perfume,
Of sacred visions, pure delight.

Each petal holds a story told,
Of journeys vast and dreams unfurled.
In nature’s arms, we dare be bold,
Transcending limits of this world.

Oh, rise beyond the mortal frame,
Embrace the heavens high above.
Through faith and love, we light the flame,
Of endless beauty, life, and love.

The stars align in cosmic grace,
Each twinkling light a guiding star.
We find ourselves in endless space,
Transforming scars to who we are.

With every breath, we weave the thread,
Connecting hearts in sacred trust.
In blooms that grow where angels tread,
We find the peace, we seek, we must.

Divine Embrace of Nature

In valleys deep, where shadows lie,
The whispers of the trees declare.
Their branches stretch towards the sky,
In nature's arms, we find our prayer.

The rivers sing of ancient tales,
Of spirits dancing in the night.
Upon the breeze, their laughter sails,
Through every heart, a spark ignites.

Beneath the stars, we gather near,
In moments woven by design.
With every sigh, the world we steer,
To seek the joy that is divine.

Oh, radiant sun, thy warmth we seek,
In fields of gold, our spirits rise.
Each gentle touch, of love unique,
In nature's heart, we find the prize.

So let us walk this sacred ground,
In harmony, our spirits soar.
In nature’s love, we all are found,
United in the heart once more.

Blossoms of the Soul

In quietude, the spirit grows,
Like tender blooms in golden light,
Each petal whispers, sweetly flows,
A breath of love, a soul's delight.

Through trials faced, our roots entwine,
In sacred soil, we find our grace,
The sacred trust, the pure divine,
In every heartbeat, find Your trace.

The blossoms sway, with gentle ease,
In harmony with heaven's song,
Together we seek to appease,
The longing heart where we belong.

With fragrant hope, we rise anew,
Embracing light, dispelling night,
In every shade, Your love shines through,
In every prayer, we seek Your sight.

Let not despair snuff out our flame,
For in the dark, Your light will gleam,
With every blossom calls Your name,
In every hope, we live the dream.

Celestial Affections

A gentle breeze, the angel's kiss,
In twilight skies where dreams take flight,
A weaving bond of sacred bliss,
In silent prayers, we find the light.

The stars align, a dance divine,
In cosmic love, the heart expands,
With every pulse, Your spark we find,
In every touch, Your guiding hands.

Through trials faced, our souls will soar,
On wings of faith, we rise and shine,
In unity, we open doors,
To realms where love and hope entwine.

Let gratitude guide every breath,
With fervent hearts, we lift our voice,
In every moment, life or death,
In Your embrace, we make our choice.

Celestial echoes, softly sing,
In chambers where the spirit grows,
As we awaken, let us bring,
A hymn of love that ever glows.

Sacred Gardens of Serenity

Within the garden, peace abounds,
In every bloom, a story told,
In sacred soil, our hearts are found,
Where love and faith shall not grow old.

The pathways paved with gentle grace,
Invite our souls to wander free,
Through fragrant fields, we seek Your face,
In every breath, Your mystery.

With hands uplifted, hearts laid bare,
We cultivate what You bestow,
In every moment, every prayer,
In sacred trust, our spirits glow.

Let kindness fall like raindrops sweet,
And nurture life in all its forms,
In unity, our hearts will meet,
Where love endures, and hope transforms.

Through trials faced, we stand with grace,
In sacred gardens, we endure,
With every heartbeat, we embrace,
In serenity, our souls are pure.

Love's Celestial Awakening

A dawn unfolds, the light appears,
Awakening hearts to love's embrace,
In whispered prayers, we cast our fears,
And shine with grace in sacred space.

In every moment, time suspends,
As souls connect, divine design,
With tender touch, the spirit mends,
In love's embrace, we intertwine.

Through trials faced, our hearts are tried,
In every storm, we find our peace,
With faith as anchor, side by side,
In love's embrace, our souls release.

Let joy abound in every song,
And lift us high in radiant light,
In love's celestial dance, we long,
To share the grace of day and night.

As stars ignite with fervent dreams,
Our spirits soar on wings of hope,
Through love, we find what truly gleams,
In every heart, the chance to cope.

Nature's Sacred Symphony

The winds whisper softly, a prayer on the breeze,
Leaves dance in rhythm, swaying with ease.
Streams sing their melodies, pure and divine,
In every sweet moment, God's light we find.

Mountains stand mighty, reaching the sky,
They cradle the heavens, where angels fly.
Colors of blossoms paint the earth wide,
In Nature's symphony, our spirits abide.

The sun bathes the world in a golden glow,
Filling our hearts with warmth, love will flow.
Clouds drift like thoughts, light and so free,
Reflecting the grace of eternity.

The night sings with stars, a celestial choir,
Illuminating paths that lift us higher.
In silence we listen, the cosmos unfold,
Nature's sacred story, in wonders retold.

Together we stand, in awe of His plight,
Listening to whispers that bring us to light.
For in every heartbeat, and every deep sigh,
We find our connection, beneath the vast sky.

Spiritual Awakening Amidst Blooms

Awake in the garden, the heart starts to bloom,
Petals unfurling, dispelling the gloom.
Sunrise brings light, a divine revelation,
In every soft whisper, a sweet transformation.

Butterflies flutter, like spirits set free,
Each color a promise of what’s meant to be.
Fragrance surrounds, a perfume of grace,
Every flower's presence, a sacred embrace.

Life's fleeting moments, a tender retreat,
Grounded in soil, our journey's complete.
Rays of compassion break through the dark,
In every small gesture, we leave our mark.

Harmony flows through the roots of the trees,
Each branch a reminder, of love that sees.
As petals fall gently, like prayers to the air,
We find our awakening, in beauty laid bare.

Together on this path, we walk hand in hand,
Trusting in growing, we learn to understand.
With open hearts shining, we seek the divine,
In the blooms of this garden, our spirits align.

Petals at the Foot of the Altar

At the altar of life, we lay down our days,
Petals of gratitude, in silent displays.
Each tear that we shed, a jewel in the night,
Reflecting our struggles, transformed into light.

With open arms raised, we gather to pray,
Offering our hopes in a delicate array.
The fragrance of faith wafts into the air,
In the stillness we feel, the presence so near.

Candles flicker softly, illuminating dreams,
Mirroring the stars, or so it seems.
In this holy space, our spirits unite,
Bound by the love that ignites in the night.

Hands reaching forward, we seek to embrace,
The beauty of life in its sacred place.
Each petal a story, a moment well spent,
At the foot of the altar, our essence is lent.

As we bow in reverence, hearts open wide,
The petals beneath us, our burdens reside.
In this sacred offering, we find the grace,
That brings us together, in love we embrace.

The Garden of Enlightened Love

In the garden of love, where spirits ignite,
Every bloom is a lesson, a guiding light.
Roses of kindness, tulips of joy,
Dancing together, no heart is a toy.

Beneath the vast sky, our hearts come alive,
In this sacred space, together we thrive.
Sunflowers reach high, seeking the sun,
In this garden of souls, we’re never undone.

Vines intertwine, unity's call,
Weakness is lifted, we rise from the fall.
The dew on the petals, a sign of our grace,
In this garden of love, we find our place.

Every whisper of wind tells stories untold,
Threads of our lives, in colors unfold.
The fragrance of togetherness, pure and so sweet,
In the garden of love, our lives are complete.

Hand in hand, we walk this blessed land,
As seeds of compassion sprout from our hands.
Together we flourish, forever entwined,
In the garden of enlightened love, we’re aligned.

Whispering Petals of Celestial Joy

In gardens where the angels sing,
Petals fall like blessings bright.
Beneath the sky, the praises ring,
A dance of grace in sacred light.

Each blossom breathes a prayer of peace,
Soft whispers carried on the breeze.
In silence, souls and hearts release,
The love that every spirit sees.

The colors tell of heavenly tales,
Of faith and hope, forever found.
Upon the winds, the spirit sails,
In every petal, love resounds.

As morning dew adorns the way,
Each droplet shines like stars above.
In every dawn, we find our stay,
In the embrace of timeless love.

So let us walk through fields of grace,
With open hearts, embrace the day.
In whispered joy, we find our place,
Amongst the blooms, our souls will sway.

The Spiritual Dance of Blossoms' Glow.

Beneath the moon's gentle embrace,
The blossoms twirl in sacred night.
In every petal, a soft trace,
Of divine love's eternal light.

The fragrant air, a hymn so pure,
Each scent a prayer that lifts on high.
In these moments, we find our cure,
In nature's grace, we learn to fly.

The currents weave a tapestry,
Of joy that fills the heart with peace.
Through every bud, a symphony,
In this dance, our sorrows cease.

As stars align in endless skies,
We gather 'neath the trees of gold.
With open hearts and lifting eyes,
We find the truths that can't be told.

In every bloom, a light will spark,
A beacon in the night's embrace.
Through whispers soft, we leave a mark,
In love's pure dance, we find our place.

Petals of Grace

In dawn's first light, the petals greet,
With hues that tell of hope anew.
They dance upon the earth's heart beat,
A chorus sung in vibrant view.

The morning whispers secrets sweet,
In gentle winds, the messages share.
As every footstep finds its beat,
We walk in faith, in love, in prayer.

Each flower blooms with stories unfold,
Of grace that flows from heaven's hand.
With every touch, the world feels bold,
In nature's grasp, we understand.

As petals fall like autumn's kiss,
We gather strength from what is shown.
In every loss, we gain our bliss,
Through love, the seeds of joy are sown.

So let us honor nature's call,
With open hearts, we bloom and grow.
In every petal, we find our all,
In grace's light, our spirits flow.

Divine Whispers of Love

In quiet moments, softly heard,
The whispers of the heart arise.
Through every leaf, a gentle word,
The love of heaven fills the skies.

Amidst the flowers, a sacred space,
Where souls connect in endless peace.
Each tender bloom reflects a face,
Of love abundant, never cease.

Through tears of joy, the petals dance,
In sunlight's warmth, they hold the dream.
In nature's grace, we find our chance,
To share our light, to let hearts beam.

The fragrance drifts, a sweet embrace,
In every breath, divine delight.
With open arms, let love encase,
Our spirits strong in love's own light.

So let us gather, hand in hand,
With grateful hearts aligned above.
In every garden, we will stand,
Embracing life, with whispers of love.

Petals of Prayer

In the quiet of dawn, we kneel,
Whispers of faith, our souls to heal.
Each petal falls, a sacred plea,
Beneath the branches, we yearn to be.

Hands folded tight, hearts open wide,
In stillness, our deepest hopes abide.
A garden blossoming in praise,
With every prayer, a love that stays.

Through trials faced, we find our grace,
In the light of love, we seek our place.
Petals carried by the gentle breeze,
In every moment, we find our ease.

The sun will rise, the shadows flee,
In unity, we choose to see.
The blossoms bloom, each one a call,
In the embrace of faith, we stand tall.

So let us gather, hand in hand,
In the heart of a sacred land.
With every prayer, we cultivate,
The petals of love that never wait.

Spiritual Flourish

In the stillness, seeds are sown,
Within our hearts, a light has grown.
A whisper stirs the soul to rise,
In faith, we lift our hopeful eyes.

The roots run deep, the branches wide,
In the sunshine, we do abide.
Each leaf a verse of love's sweet song,
In unity, we all belong.

Through trials faced and darkness near,
We find our strength, dispelling fear.
In every moment, grace will flow,
A spiritual bloom, we come to know.

Together, we will seek and find,
The treasure of a gentle mind.
A flourish born from love's embrace,
In every heart, a sacred space.

So let us grow with every breath,
In the cycle of life, conquering death.
With hope as our guide, we step ahead,
In spiritual flourish, our hearts are fed.

Seeds of Divine Love

In the depths of the earth, seeds lie,
Waiting for rain from a soft sky.
With each drop, a promise bestowed,
In the warmth of light, their life flowed.

Each sprout unfolds, a miracle clear,
In the garden of hearts, we find cheer.
With tendrils reaching for sky above,
In every heartbeat, we share love.

Through whispers of wind, they are stirred,
In the silence, divine truth is heard.
From the ground, to the heavens, they climb,
In the rhythm of life, a sacred rhyme.

With each bloom, a story of grace,
In the presence of God, we find our place.
The seeds we sow, in heart and mind,
In the soil of faith, our lives entwined.

So let us plant with hands held high,
In every moment, let love not die.
With every heartbeat, our spirits weave,
Seeds of divine love, we shall believe.

The Garden of Inner Peace

In the stillness of night, peace descends,
Whispers of calm, where the spirit mends.
In the garden of silence, we find our way,
To the heart of the night, where shadows sway.

Each petal soft, a reminder clear,
That in quiet moments, love draws near.
With every breath, we cultivate grace,
An oasis of hope, a tranquil space.

Through trials faced and storms that roar,
In the stillness, we seek for more.
The garden blooms, a gentle sight,
In the arms of faith, we find our light.

So nurture the soil of your sacred heart,
In the garden of peace, let love impart.
With roots that hold, and branches that sway,
In the haven of stillness, may we stay.

For the garden, it whispers, a sweet refrain,
In the presence of love, we rise again.
So let us gather, beneath the skies,
In the garden of inner peace, where the spirit flies.

The Altar of Tender Sprouts

In gardens lush where spirit grows,
Beneath the sun, the gentle prose,
Life unfolds in sacred light,
As love's embrace ignites the night.

With every leaf, a prayer takes flight,
A hum of faith, the heart's delight,
In soil rich, our hopes are sown,
To harvest joy, we stand as one.

The roots entwine, divinely bound,
In tranquil moments, solace found,
Each droplet of dew, a holy sign,
Of love's pure grace, a gift divine.

Let whispers of the breezes sing,
Of tender shoots and what they bring,
For in each bloom, a truth unfolds,
A tale of mercy, softly told.

So gather near, as faith takes form,
In every sprout, a spirit warm,
Together, let's our voices raise,
In gratitude, with hearts ablaze.

Unfolding Petals of Grace

With morning's light, the petals sway,
A dance of faith, a bright array,
In fragrant breaths, the spirits meet,
In gentle whispers, love is sweet.

Each blossom's heart, a story shared,
Of trials faced and burdens bared,
With open arms, we find our place,
In arms of love, in purest grace.

The colors sing of mercy's hue,
In symphonies of me and you,
And as we bloom in sacred ties,
We rise, uplifted, toward the skies.

In stillness found, beneath the tree,
The shade of hope, it cradles me,
Unfolding dreams in soft embrace,
As we partake in love's own pace.

Let every petal, tender, glide,
Upon the winds where spirits bide,
For in this garden, souls entwine,
In petals soft, the pure divine.

Reverent Whispers of Amour

In the quiet hush of evening’s glow,
Where stars align and rivers flow,
Faith's whispers weave a sacred thread,
A tapestry of love, widely spread.

With every sigh, a gentle vow,
To honor here, and then, and now,
In tender glances, hearts exposed,
In reverence shared, the truth composed.

As shadows dance on twilight’s face,
We find our peace in love’s embrace,
In every heartbeat, prayers reside,
In trust’s soft language, hearts collide.

The moonlight spills on paths we've shared,
A guiding light, for souls compared,
In whispers soft, our spirits soar,
Together, forever, we explore.

So lift your voice and let it rise,
With every word, with every sigh,
In murmurs pure, our love expressed,
In sacred stillness, we are blessed.

Celestial Seeds of Compassion

In every heart, a seed is sown,
With tender care, it's gently grown,
Through acts of love, we break the ground,
In unity, our hopes abound.

The cosmic dance of grace unfurls,
As compassion spreads, it twirls and twirls,
For in our hands, a sacred quest,
To nurture souls and give our best.

With open arms, we greet the day,
In kindness shared, we light the way,
Each gentle word, a ray of sun,
Together, we are ever one.

In moments pure, divine reflections,
Celestial bonds, our true connections,
For as we sow the seeds of care,
We reap the love, in every prayer.

So let us tread on holy ground,
With every pulse, our hearts resound,
For in this life, with grace we'll stand,
In seeds of love, we make our brand.

Love's Ethereal Garden

In the garden where love resides,
Hearts entwined beneath the skies.
Petals whisper, soft and sweet,
In every bloom, His grace we meet.

Stars above, our witness bright,
Guiding souls in sacred night.
Through trials, we shall always grow,
In love's embrace, our spirits flow.

From roots of faith, our bond does rise,
Nurtured by the light that ties.
With every breath, we plant anew,
A sacred space, just me and you.

As seasons change and time unfolds,
In love's garden, truth beholds.
Together, hand in hand we stand,
Forever blessed, our hearts expand.

In joy and sorrow, love will stay,
Guiding us along the way.
In this garden, pure and true,
Love's ethereal grace shines through.

The Blooming Light of Faith

In dawn's embrace, the light is born,
A beacon bright, our hearts adorn.
With trust as roots, we reach for skies,
In faith we rise, our spirits fly.

Each moment shines a sacred hue,
In love's reflection, we walk through.
The shadows flee, our fears unwind,
In every prayer, a peace we find.

The world may tremble, storms may rage,
Yet faith will turn a brand new page.
With open hearts, we seek the way,
In every night, there comes a day.

Through trials faced, our bond shall grow,
In unity, the love we show.
The blooming light shall lead our path,
In grace, we'll learn to share His wrath.

For every tear, there is a bloom,
Transforming darkness into room.
In hope we walk, side by side,
With faith our guide, in Him we bide.

Blooming Vows

In sacred vows, our souls unite,
Promises whispered in the night.
With gentle hands, our hearts we bind,
In love's embrace, true peace we find.

With every beat, our love takes flight,
A melody of pure delight.
Through life's journey, come what may,
Together, let our spirits sway.

In laughter shared and tears we've cried,
In every storm, we'll be the tide.
Through fire and ice, our bond will stand,
In bloom and grace, we hold the hand.

Each moment framed in sacred light,
Above the shadows, love ignites.
With words that echo from above,
We'll build a life, entwined in love.

As seasons change and time unfurls,
In every breath, our love swirls.
With blooming vows, we start anew,
Each day's promise, just me and you.

In the Hands of the Creator

In hands divine, our lives are spun,
We walk in light, our journey begun.
With purpose clear, our hearts align,
In love's embrace, His grace we find.

Every breath a gift, we share,
In fields of joy, we find Him there.
Through valleys low and mountains high,
With faith as wings, we learn to fly.

In every challenge, love will bloom,
Dispelling shadows, chasing gloom.
For in His hands, we are not lost,
In every trial, love's worth the cost.

Together we walk, side by side,
In His embrace, there's naught to hide.
With hearts as one, our spirits soar,
In creation's arms, we long for more.

Through chaos and calm, we shall remain,
In His design, our love's the gain.
In the hands of the Creator's grace,
We find our peace, a holy place.

Sacred Seed of Love

In the heart's garden, a seed is sown,
Watered with faith, in silence it's grown.
Nurtured by kindness, it reaches for light,
A bloom of compassion to banish the night.

In whispers of prayer, its petals unfold,
A tapestry woven, each thread a tale told.
With roots deeply anchored in grace and in trust,
It stands through the tempest, steadfast and just.

Each morning it greets the bright sun in cheer,
A symbol of love that conquers all fear.
In the eyes of the humble, it shines ever bright,
The sacred seed vibrant, a beacon of light.

So tend to this garden where love's spirit thrives,
Where joy intertwines and the soul truly strives.
For in sharing its bounty, we gather as one,
In the sacred dance of love, we are never undone.

Let faith be the soil, and hope be the rain,
In the blossoming beauty, we echo its name.
The sacred seed of love, forever shall bloom,
In the hearts of the faithful, dispelling all gloom.

Blossoms of Piety

In the dew-kissed morn, the blossoms arise,
Fragrant and pure beneath heavenly skies.
Each petal a prayer, each leaf a soft sigh,
A chorus of praises that reaches up high.

Through valleys of sorrow, they bravely stand tall,
In unity's garden, they answer the call.
With colors of mercy and shades of delight,
They draw the lost souls back into the light.

With roots intertwined in a covenant strong,
They sway to the rhythm of hope's gentle song.
In the arms of the faithful, they flourish and grow,
In the dance of devotion, they radiate glow.

Each blossom a promise, of peace and of grace,
Filling the world with love's vibrant embrace.
In the shadow of trials, they bloom ever bright,
The blossoms of piety, a testament of light.

So gather their fragrance in hearts that believe,
In moments of doubt, let their beauty weave.
For in each soft petal, divine whispers are sown,
In the garden of faith, we are never alone.

The Altar of Petals

At the altar of petals, we gather with grace,
Offering thanks for this sacred place.
In silence we kneel, hearts open in prayer,
Beneath the watchful gaze of the skies so rare.

The fragrance of devotion, a sweet perfume,
Lifts our spirits upward, dispelling all gloom.
With each heartfelt whisper, a petal we lay,
In honor of love that guides all our way.

The colors united, a mosaic of trust,
Reflecting the light of the Divine that we must.
In the depth of our souls, the truth we embrace,
In the warmth of compassion, we find our own space.

Each moment a blessing, each breath a decree,
In the tapestry woven, we find unity.
The altar of petals, where hearts intertwine,
A sanctuary built on love, pure and divine.

So cherish the moments, let gratitude sing,
For life is a gift, and in joy we take wing.
At the altar of petals, together we rise,
In the light of our faith, we transcend to the skies.

Celestial Flourish

In the realm of the heavens, a flourish takes flight,
With whispers of love, it dances in light.
Stars twinkle as blessings, a celestial song,
In the embrace of creation, where all hearts belong.

The cosmos adorns us with treasures so rare,
Each twinkle a promise, each moment a prayer.
In the grandeur of night, our spirits expand,
United in faith, in the Divine's gentle hand.

Through trials and triumphs, we flourish and grow,
Like blossoms of light in a celestial show.
With love as our anchor, we reach for the skies,
In the arms of the cosmos, our souls ever rise.

So gather the stardust, let dreams intertwine,
In the tapestry woven, our fates align.
With hearts as our guides, we navigate space,
In this celestial flourish, we find our true place.

Each moment a gift, each heartbeat a chance,
To cherish the love in this heavenly dance.
With grace in our steps, towards the light we dash,
In the celestial flourish, let us everlast.

Hearts Like Lilies

In fields where lilies bloom so bright,
Hearts gather 'neath the golden light.
With every petal, grace descends,
In silent whispers, love transcends.

The fragrance of faith fills the air,
Each blossom tells us He is there.
With roots entwined in loamy earth,
We find our strength, our holy worth.

Through stormy trials, we stand tall,
Like lilies rising after all.
In unity, we lift our voice,
In sacred trust, we make our choice.

With tender hearts, we seek the way,
In every dawn, a new display.
Our souls adorned, in beauty's dress,
In His embrace, we find our rest.

So let our hearts, like lilies stand,
In every moment, hand in hand.
Grounded deep in love's embrace,
Together we uplift our grace.

Sacred Verses in Petals

Each petal holds a sacred word,
In every breeze, His voice is heard.
As nature weaves its tapestry,
We find His truth in mystery.

In gardens where the faithful pray,
The blossoms dance in bright array.
With every hue, a hymn is sung,
In languages of old, we've sprung.

We gather hopes, like dew at dawn,
In faith's embrace, our worries gone.
The sun illuminates the night,
In sacred verses, our hearts write.

We tread on paths of love and grace,
With open eyes, we seek His face.
In every flower, a story told,
Of endless love, of life, of gold.

So together, let our spirits soar,
In unity, we seek Him more.
With petals soft, we cling to prayer,
In sacred verses, His love we share.

Flourishing in Spirit's Embrace

In every breath, a sacred peace,
We find in Him our sweet release.
As blossoms bloom in radiant light,
Flourishing souls, we take our flight.

The Spirit's touch ignites the flame,
In every heart, we feel the same.
With open arms, we gather close,
In this divine love, we engross.

With gratitude, our voices rise,
Like morning songs that fill the skies.
In the garden of His grace,
We flourish in our rightful place.

Through trials faced, we stand together,
In faith and love, we can't sever.
With every trial, a lesson learned,
In Spirit's embrace, we're everturned.

So let our hearts be intertwined,
In every moment, love aligned.
Together we shall bloom and grow,
In Spirit's warmth, forever glow.

The Divine Bouquet

A bouquet bright with colors rare,
Each bloom a token of His care.
In petals soft, His mercy shines,
In grace-filled hearts, His love aligns.

With every stem, a story shared,
In gentle whispers, we are bared.
Like flowers swaying in the wind,
Our souls in Him, forever pinned.

As nature sings a hymn of hope,
In unity, we learn to cope.
Together woven, strong and bold,
In faith's bouquet, our dreams unfold.

Each blossom teaches us to give,
In sharing love, we truly live.
With gratitude, our hearts impart,
The essence of His holy heart.

So let us cherish every bloom,
In life's grand garden, there's no gloom.
With hands embraced, our spirits free,
In divine bouquet, we are He.

Sacred Harmony in Bloom

In the garden of faith, we stand still,
Whispers of hope in the air we fill.
Petals unfold under heaven's gaze,
Guided by love through life's winding maze.

Hands lifted high, hearts open wide,
In this divine space, we shall abide.
Each moment a gift, embraced with grace,
In sacred harmony, we find our place.

Nature sings softly, a celestial tune,
Under the watchful eye of the moon.
Sunlight pours forth, a radiant beam,
Awakening souls to a shared dream.

Presence of spirit in every breath drawn,
With gratitude bursting at each dawn.
Blossoms of faith, nourished by tears,
Blooming in beauty, casting out fears.

Together we rise, as one, side by side,
In the dance of creation, where love is our guide.
Embracing the sacred through joy and strife,
In harmony's arms, we celebrate life.

Fragrant Offerings to the Divine

With hands full of blossoms, we lift our voice,
In the presence of grace, we gladly rejoice.
Each petal a whisper, each scent a prayer,
Fragrant offerings sent into the air.

In stillness we ponder, with hearts open wide,
A tapestry woven, with faith as our guide.
Glistening dew drops, like tears from above,
Nurturing seeds of compassion and love.

Breathe in the sweetness of life's gentle flow,
Exhale the burdens, let worries go.
In the sacred circle, we gather as one,
Embracing the warmth of the rising sun.

With every flower that bids us to see,
The beauty of being, the joy to be free.
Offering ourselves in the spirit of grace,
In fragrant devotion, we find our place.

As seasons keep turning, our spirits entwine,
In love's gentle fragrance, we know we are divine.
With faith as our compass, we journey along,
Each fragrant offering, a love-filled song.

Blossoms of Graceful Abandon

In the meadow of moments, we dance and we sway,
Blossoms of grace greet the dawning day.
With petals unfurling, our spirits take flight,
In abandonment's beauty, we find our light.

The gentle breeze whispers, sweet melodies play,
Calling us deeper, inviting to stay.
We bask in the warmth of the sun's golden rays,
Trusting the journey, through life's winding ways.

With open hearts ready, we welcome the flow,
As flowers in bloom, our love starts to grow.
In every soft sigh, in every warm glance,
We gather together in divine cosmic dance.

Each moment a heartbeat, each heartbeat a song,
In the embrace of the holy, we all belong.
With spirits entwined in the rhythm of grace,
In blossoms of love, we find our true place.

Through trials and triumphs, we remain unafraid,
For in graceful abandon, our fears start to fade.
United in purpose, our souls intertwine,
In the garden of life, forever we shine.

Threads of Divine Connectivity

Woven in silence, our hearts intertwine,
Threads of connection, a tapestry divine.
Each soul a strand in this sacred embrace,
Bound by the love that time cannot erase.

In moments of stillness, our spirits align,
A gentle reminder, in faith we define.
With threads of compassion, we weave through the night,

Stitching together our dreams in the light.

As rivers of mercy flow deep and wide,
In the fabric of kindness, we gracefully glide.
Each knot tells a story, of joy and of pain,
In threads of connection, we dance in the rain.

With hands that uplift, and voices that sing,
United, we blossom like flowers in spring.
In the warmth of togetherness, love lights the way,
We honor the threads that keep darkness at bay.

So join in the weaving, together we'll stand,
In the threads of the divine, a united hand.
For every connection is sacred and true,
In this bright tapestry, there's always room for you.

Divine Petals of Affection

In the whispering dawn, love unfolds,
Grace drapes the earth in colors bold.
Heaven's breath stirs each tender bloom,
As hearts entwine, dispelling gloom.

Soft petals drift on a holy breeze,
While angels hum in joyous ease.
Each fragile bloom holds a prayer sincere,
Woven with whispers for all to hear.

Sunshine kisses the blossoms fair,
Bathed in light, they spark the air.
In every color, a story told,
Of divine affection, pure and gold.

United in faith, the flowers sway,
In a sacred dance, they freely play.
Their beauty speaks of a love profound,
In this garden, grace is found.

With every petal, a promise bright,
Guiding souls toward inner light.
In the embrace of these fragrant sights,
Divine affection ignites the nights.

Sacred Blossoms of the Soul

In the silence of night, soft petals gleam,
Blooming with hope, like a sacred dream.
Each bud whispers secrets of the divine,
Illuminating paths that forever shine.

Through shadowed woods, where spirits sing,
The sacred blooms of love take wing.
Their fragrance drifts on the holy air,
Inviting souls with gentle care.

With uplifted hearts, we kneel in awe,
Embracing the beauty of ancient law.
In every blossom, a truth revealed,
Our souls united, forever sealed.

Mirrors of faith in the light's embrace,
In nature's bounty, we find our place.
Through trials faced, our spirits grow,
In sacred blossoms, love's rivers flow.

As dawn paints the sky with tender hue,
We gather the wisdom of the flowers anew.
With gratitude rising, our voices soar,
In this sacred dance, we become evermore.

The Garden of Devotion

At the heart of stillness, a garden glows,
Where devotion sprouts like the softest rose.
Each leaf and petal, a heartfelt vow,
As we seek grace in the here and now.

Under the arch of the ancient trees,
Whispers of love float upon the breeze.
In the roots, a sacred history lies,
Where every blossom reaches for the skies.

With gentle hands, we tend the soil,
Nourishing faith through humble toil.
In every seed of hope we sow,
A promise blooms, destined to grow.

In this hallowed space, we find our way,
Each fragrant moment, a gift of the day.
The garden flourishes with silent prayer,
In the hearts of those who wander there.

Sunrise breaks with a golden glow,
Painting the petals, urging them to grow.
In the garden of devotion, we belong,
Where love's sweet melody writes our song.

Embrace of Celestial Fragrance

In twilight's arms, the fragrances blend,
Flowers of faith, as spirits ascend.
Each scent a whisper of love divine,
Binding our souls in a holy line.

With petals soft as the moonlit night,
They beckon us into the sacred light.
In every blossom, a celestial grin,
Awakening hearts as the journey begins.

From the depths of the earth, they rise high,
Reaching for heaven like dreams in the sky.
In the hum of creation, they sing, they sway,
Celebrating love in each wondrous display.

Treading lightly on this cherished ground,
In the embrace of fragrance, we are found.
Where echoes of prayer in the air convene,
A tapestry woven with love's sheen.

As twilight deepens, stars start to glow,
In fragrant gardens where seekers go.
Bound by devotion, our spirits sing,
In the embrace of love, all souls take wing.

Blooming in the Light of Faith

In the garden of belief, we stand,
Nurtured by grace, guided by hand.
Each flower a whisper of sacred trust,
In shadows of doubt, we rise from dust.

With petals that glisten, in morning's glow,
Hearts lifted high, as soft winds blow.
The sun shines down on the path we tread,
Illuminating hopes, where angels tread.

Faith blooms eternal, through trials we face,
In the deep of night, we seek His grace.
Roots intertwined, in love we find,
A symphony of souls, in Him aligned.

Each blossom tells stories of mercy and light,
In the embrace of hope, we conquer the night.
With fragrant whispers, we offer our praise,
In the light of faith, we spend our days.

So let us be bold, like the blooms we see,
In the garden of love, forever free.
Together we flourish, in unity bound,
In the light of faith, true joy is found.

The Petal Pathway to Divine

Upon the petals, our prayers take flight,
Carried on breezes through the still night.
Each step we take on this sacred route,
Leads us to blessings no words can tout.

In velvet whispers, the flowers speak,
Of hope and faith, in moments meek.
With dew-kissed dreams, our spirits rise,
Under the canopy of endless skies.

The pathway woven with love and grace,
Inviting us gently to seek His face.
Each bud that opens reveals a sign,
Of the divine love that ever aligns.

As colors blend in harmonious song,
We find our strength where we belong.
Step by step, hearts open wide,
On the petal pathway, we walk beside.

Together we wander, hand in hand,
In the realm of faith, a sacred land.
Through fragrant meadows, we will proceed,
In the light of love, we plant the seed.

The Madonna's Garden

In the garden of grace, the Madonna waits,
With love that enfolds, healing our fates.
Each bloom a promise, each leaf a prayer,
In her gentle embrace, we find solace rare.

Her hands weave hope in the softest embrace,
In the silence of beauty, we seek her face.
With tender strength, she guides our way,
In the Madonna’s garden, we wish to stay.

The lilies of faith rise, pure and bright,
Bathed in the warmth of her nurturing light.
Amid the blossoms, we gather near,
In her loving presence, we conquer fear.

With every petal that falls to the ground,
A reminder of love that ever surrounds.
In the stillness of night, we hear her song,
In the Madonna's garden, we all belong.

So let us remember the path she shows,
Through trials of life, sweet love bestows.
Forever we’re blessed in her gentle care,
In the heart of the garden, true love is rare.

A Bouquet of Faithful Promises

A bouquet of faith, with colors bright,
Each petal a promise, a beacon of light.
In trials and sorrow, we stand as one,
Hand in hand, beneath the sun.

With every fragrance, we hear the call,
A symphony of hope, lifting us all.
As the flowers bloom, so does our grace,
In the garden of faith, we find our place.

Each blossom a testament, night turns to day,
In the warmth of His love, we learn to pray.
Through the cradling arms of the gentle wind,
Our hearts are renewed, as we begin.

In this sacred space, we share our dreams,
With whispers of love flowing in streams.
Together we flourish, entwined in trust,
In the bouquet of promises, we rise from dust.

Let our hearts sing out in harmonious blend,
With faith as our guide, on Him we depend.
In the garden of life, may our spirits soar,
With a bouquet of promises, forevermore.

The Divine Blooming of Spirit

In gardens where silence breathes,
The spirit unfolds like petals wide,
Awakening softly with morning's light,
A sacred whisper, a gentle guide.

Each bloom bears witness to grace divine,
Colors entwined in holy embrace,
A tapestry woven with love so pure,
In the heart of a garden, we find our place.

Through trials we rise and bend not low,
Roots digging deep in the soil of faith,
As heavens pour blessings, we shall grow,
In the warmth of Love's radiant wraith.

The fragrance of prayer fills the air,
Notes of devotion entwine like vines,
In the dance of our spirits united,
We bloom ever bright where Light aligns.

So let us gather where lilies sing,
In the meadow of faith, we stand as one,
Hands lifted high as offerings rise,
In the dawn of our spirit, the journey's begun.

Flowers of the Covenant

In fields of promise, we take our stand,
Each flower a pact, a love solo,
With petals that whisper, 'We understand,'
A bond of trust in the seeds we sow.

Each blossom tells stories of trials past,
Of faith that flourished in storms' embrace,
Through seasons of sorrow, joy steadfast,
In the tapestry of time, we find our grace.

In the fragrance of blooming, a sacred song,
Echoes of spirits harmonizing bright,
Together we grow, where we belong,
Nurtured in kindness, sheltered in light.

As rains cleanse the earth and sun warms the heart,
We walk in the garden with souls aligned,
Woven together, we shall not part,
In Love's rich covenant, eternally bind.

In the bounty of blossoms our hopes shall stay,
A symphony of colors, in faith we bloom,
With each petal unfolding, we pave the way,
For a world renewed in Love's fragrant room.

Blooming in the Light of Prayer

In the stillness where quiet reigns,
Hearts awaken to the soft refrain,
With hands uplifted, we seek the skies,
In the light of prayer, our spirit flies.

Each whisper, a seed in sacred ground,
Nurtured by faith, where hope is found,
In the warmth of grace, our essence grows,
In the garden of hearts, the divine bestows.

As shadows retreat with dawn's gentle glow,
We bask in the warmth of love's soft flow,
Together we'll rise, as flowers do,
In the bloom of prayer, our lives renew.

With every heartbeat, a melody sweet,
In the symphony of prayer, our souls meet,
United in love, we blossom and shine,
In the tapestry woven, the joy is divine.

So let us gather in harmony's nest,
With hearts full of hope and souls truly blessed,
Together we blossom, in peace we lay,
In the light of prayer, we find our way.

Sacred Roots of Connection

Beneath the surface where life takes hold,
Roots intertwine, a story bold,
In the soil of faith, we nurture the ground,
In sacred connection, our hearts are found.

Through trials endured, we strengthen our ties,
With whispers of love, in silence we rise,
The bonds that we forge, unseen and true,
In the garden of souls, we bloom anew.

As each season passes, the cycle remains,
The power of love in our hearts sustains,
With every connection, the spirit expands,
A tapestry woven by divine hands.

In unity's embrace, our roots reach wide,
Drawing strength from each other, side by side,
In the sacred dance of life, we trust,
In Love's gentle whisper, our hearts adjust.

So let us remember the ground where we stand,
In the arms of connection, we lend a hand,
Together we flourish, with love as our guide,
In the sacred roots of life, we abide.

Fragrance of the Divine

In gardens lush, the lilies sway,
Their fragrance whispers soft and low,
A testament to love and grace,
In every petal, pure light glows.

The rose unfolds, in colors bright,
With thorns to guard its sacred peace,
Each bloom a prayer, a sacred rite,
In Nature's heart, our souls release.

Through fragrant earth, the spirits dance,
With every breeze, a holy song,
The heavens smile, a sweet romance,
Where life and love have lived so long.

Beneath the stars, in twilight's calm,
The flowers bow, their heads in prayer,
In harmony, they weave a psalm,
A fragrance of the Divine, so rare.

O Holy Gardener, hear our plea,
Nurture this ground, let kindness bloom,
For in Your grace, we long to see,
The fragrance that dispels all gloom.

The Growing Promise

In gentle soil, a seedling stirs,
Awakening to warmth and light,
A promise forged through silent words,
In shadows, it finds strength to fight.

With every drop of rain's embrace,
The roots delve deep, they strive and yearn,
Through cycles of the sun's own race,
From dark to dawn, the lessons learned.

The budding leaves, their green unfurls,
A life reborn in vibrant hue,
Each breath a gift, as time whirls,
In Nature's heart, old dreams renew.

Through storms that rage, the branches bend,
Yet wisdom grows from trials faced,
With faith, the journey has no end,
Each moment kissed by love's embrace.

O Spirit of the growing seed,
Guide us through life's tangled maze,
In every challenge, plant the creed,
That promise bright shall light our days.

Grace in Every Bloom

In every flower, grace unfolds,
A testament to hands divine,
Each color tells of love untold,
In beauty wrapped, the heart aligns.

The daisy sings in fields of green,
A simple joy, pure innocence,
A smile from God, serene, unseen,
In harmony, we find our sense.

When violets peep from winter's shroud,
They whisper tales of hope reborn,
Through trials faced, we stand unbowed,
In every bloom, new life is sworn.

Through petals soft, the spirit soars,
In fragrant air, we breathe anew,
The sacred dance of cosmic shores,
In every bloom, God's love rings true.

O Giver of the sacred art,
Let us reflect Your truth and light,
In every bloom, our faithful heart,
Shall find our way from dark to bright.

Serenity's Floral Embrace

In quiet gardens, time stands still,
Where blossoms breathe in whispered peace,
Each petal held with tender will,
In every bud, life’s sweet release.

The lavender sways, a soothing balm,
Its scent a prayer that calms the soul,
In fragrant fields, we find our calm,
In Nature's arms, we become whole.

The marigold reflects the sun,
With vibrant hues, it shares its grace,
In every touch, a life begun,
In every glance, love's warm embrace.

When evening falls, and shadows creep,
The night blooms whisper soft and low,
A promise kept, as dreams we weave,
In serenity's gentle glow.

O Lord of Nature, hear our plea,
In every flower, let us find,
A tranquil heart, a love set free,
In floral grace, our souls entwined.

Milton Keynes UK
Ingram Content Group UK Ltd.
UKHW031321271124
451618UK00007B/161

9 789916 898321